The right of Crispin to be identified as the author of this
work has been asserted in accordance with Section 78
of the Copyright, Designs and Patents Act 1988

The book cover is copyright to Crispin

This book is published by
Grosvenor House Publishing Ltd
Link House
140 The Broadway, Tolworth, Surrey, KT6 7HT.
www.grosvenorhousepublishing.co.uk

A CIP record for this book
is available from the British Library

ISBN 978-1-83975-491-3

Poeticus Pictoralis

A small form of daffodil named "Poet's narcissi"
and a style of painting that enhances the beauty
of the subject.

A book of 60 natural, humorous and
philosophical poems.

By
Crispin

With original art from his family.

**Grosvenor House
Publishing Limited**

Attributions

All poems have been written by me.

The artwork is by:

Mary's art is front & rear cover and pages 3, 37, 53 & 91

Angie's art is pages 41, 55 & 83

Jane's art is pages 11, 25, 33, 45 and the 60 image

Vic's art is pages 13, 19, 31, 35, 49, 95 & 99

Crispin's art is pages 29, 61 & 65

Dedications

This humble book of poetry is dedicated with grateful thanks to:

My dear father, John (sadly missed), who gave me the gift of words.

My dear mother, Mary, who has always encouraged me to be creative.

My dear and lovely wife, Angie, who helped me understand love.

My dear, clever and artistic daughters, Jane & Vic… I'm always impressed.

My friends and colleagues in the Bristol Regional office, who always said I should publish my poetry (here it is Karen).

Also, my good friend, colleague and golfing buddy Mike.

Colourful Quotes

I'm not aware of any crime, necessitating doing time?

His bitter handsome features, clearly did reflect, his loathing of the skill I'd shown and maybe some respect.

The canvas sails soaking, flapping and wet, like a fish starved of water, in oxygen debt.

The sun-soaked day and sultry moon-bathed night.

The fruit of labour gifts the grateful heart.

Rhythmic, repeating, like the clock of the world, a billion tons of water, onto the land is hurled.

And make the planet's health your wedding ring.

In country law, this simple truth was gifted to my curious youth.

The pigeons scatter like an icy fountain's blast.

For what are we? Any of us, but memory's construct?

The blades of my sword, earthly fortunes anoint.

Grizzled grey bark, furrowed tracks for busy insect feet.

Shrinking ear from shrieking child.

I burst away, adrenalin, the food of flight, my limbs were strong, my body, youthful, light.

For the journey from our nothingness to the state of being born,
Is chaperoned and possibly by the same unfathomable form.

The forest ponies, free to wander and to graze,
Appear to ripple, with the rising heat of summer haze,

The artist in a leap of faith, applies the early paint,
Like childhood, this is learning and so, the strokes are faint.

Index of contents

INDEX

Nature poems

Rounding the yellow buoy

Feel the boat pitch and feel the boat yaw,
The wind is a constant and that constant is
  raw,
The boat is bucking, as though it's alive,
Hang on…it's your lifeline, the means to
  survive,

The swell of the wave lifts your little-planked
  boat,
In the abyss now below you, a glimpse of…
  petticoat,
For the sea is your mistress… life, longing and
  love,
Her power on earth, made in the heavens
  above,

The ropes of the sail, chime rapidly on the
  mast,
A tune without rhythm, a tune that beats fast,
A crazy cacophony of percussion and strings,
Your face is screwed up, as the salt sea-spray
  stings,

Round the yellow buoy and tack your way
  home,
To the left, to the right, ride the white foam,
The canvas sails, soaking, flapping and wet,
Like a fish starved of water, in oxygen debt,

At last, your prow has grooved the sand,
Your sailing partner has proffered their hand,
Smiles at last crease your salty faces,
As you look with affection upon dangerous
    places,

Bring the sail down, wash all with clean water,
You've challenged the sea. You have loved her
    and fought her,
The wind was her anger. The waves were her
    mood,
Now remember her fondly as you go to get
    food.

Hedge

Long-time planted, rough and slanted, it dustily
    marks the edge,
Of fields of grass and serpentine paths, behind
    the bristly hedge,
Octopus arms of thorny bramble barbs, whip
    with wind-fuelled motion,
Berries and roots and curative shoots, could be
    gathered for a potion,

Ripe and round, blackberries found, like dog's
    black pastel noses,
Flowers compete, to furnish a treat, cowslips
    and poppies and roses,
Butterflies land, like an old shaking hand and
    applaud with their wings on their backs,
Little field mice are gone in a trice, desperate
    to cover their tracks,

Mushrooms abound, in the damp sheltered
    ground, loving the dark by the roots,
While climbers coil, in an attempt to foil,
    competitor's up-thrusting shoots,
All this is found, in the margins of ground,
    though its value is abundantly clear,
Our last chance to cherish, what must never
    perish, approaches us quickly, I fear.

One moment

A fur-clad bee clambers over the flowering
   clover,
A butterfly jiggles by, as if hung upon a
   puppet's strings,
A dragonfly is mirrored in the pond it hovers
   over,
With petrol colours shimmering on its vibrating
   nouveau wings,

A fox appears, his head held low before him,
The pigeons scatter like an icy fountain's blast,
The flowers, with bonnets bright and waists so
   slim,
Embrace the Sun's warm blessing like it will be
   their last.

Bournemouth, Christchurch, Poole

Seven miles of golden, sandy, beach,
The Conqueror's new forest is there, in easy
    reach,
The forest ponies, free to wander and to graze,
Appear to ripple, with the rising heat of
    summer haze,

Christchurch Priory, a millennium has nearly
    passed,
The tall grey stone, cold beauty, chambers
    vast,
A walking prayer feels natural and complete,
Pass silently, the tombs beneath your feet,

The quayside Poole, fresh fish are still, here
    landed,
Little boat ties up, salty wet rope and
    fisherman leather-handed,
Takes his pots and bags of writhing catch,
Then sells it fresh to you, from his cabin,
    through a hatch,

Hop aboard a ferryboat, to Brownsea you
    should head,
An island in the harbour, green trees and
    squirrels red,
Owned and run by Baden-Powell, (his statue
    now in hiding),
A perfect place for boys to scout and girls to do
    their guiding,

The sand at Branksome beach is soft and
   honey gold,
Bright and stripy deckchairs, give comfort to
   the old,
Who smile in wistful memory, as their Youngers
   swim and play,
And remember far off summers, just like it was
   today.

The years

As years pass me like seagulls sailing in the
  gusting wind,
And life moves on, the cycle of happenings
  wheeling by,
The knowledge grows that one's ticket will
  rescind,
And all shall fade from this appreciative eye,

The spring, when green is light and firm and
  bursting through,
The Flyers nest and set about making next
  year's team,
The scenery is painting itself anew,
And all the world is full of the brand new
  (ancient) dream,

The summer, when things are at their height,
And all who can, enjoy life to the full,
The sun-soaked day and sultry moon-bathed
  night,
It never ends, but I know it always will,

Autumn comes and summer seems extended,
The fruit of labour gifts the grateful heart,
Somehow here, the joy feels somewhat ended,
Though nearer the end, the nearer to the start,

Winter stamps his muddy boots upon our rug,
And challenges all to see his tenure through,
He makes us wrap up against him, warm and
     snug,
As he decorates the twiggy trees with icy dew,

For lucky ones this cycle is repeated,
Many times and different every time,
For me, as I write this, thoughtful and seated,
I thank the Lord, it's wonderful and it's mine.

Sea

I stand and the wind strokes and slaps my
   willing face,
My soul is transported to another place,
That place is here and exactly now, but also
   then and time to come,
The sea does this to me and more and then
   some,

Hear the curling waves hook and claw the
   heavy shore,
Pulling all it can into itself and wanting more,
Rhythmic, repeating like the clock of the world,
A billion tons of water onto the land is hurled,

Out there in the deep dark water, alien worlds
   are grown,
Family of this planet, familiar yet unknown,
Creatures of mysterious design and action,
Scare me, yet fill me with strange attraction,

No amount of time spent by the sea is wasted,
I'm addicted to the timeless thoughts I've
   tasted,
If spirit I become when my mortal life is
   through,
Looking Seaward I will be, until I'm back with
   you.

Walking in the lane

I had visited a Customer in the Hampshire
   countryside,
It was a few miles north of Winchester, where
   the wealthy folk reside,
I had time to kill before the time I was due at
   my next meeting,
So, I parked the car, opened the box and
   promptly started eating.

I saw the scene around me was rustic, green
   and pretty,
So very far from the hectic scenes of village,
   town and city,
I walked away from HEF (my car), happy in his
   lay-by,
No parking pressure, or ticket required, or time
   you have to pay by,

I walked along the empty lane and saw above
   me wheeling,
A giant bird of (you'd better pray) and flesh he
   was for stealing,
His wings were outward from his body, as he
   circled in hunting rings,
His eagle eye was working hard as he rode his
   giant wings.

I'd seen him earlier from the car, in a less
   majestic engagement,
A fierce and angry jet black crow, attacked him
   through enragement,

The crow would show a greater skill, swooping, striking, swerving,
In a clinch, the crow would lose, of course, but a lesson he was serving,

In the hedgerow to my right, a rustling amongst the leaves,
I stop and listen and look a while, a mouse, he barely breathes,
I heard the rustle several times as I walked for a country mile,
Hiding from the flying death... Is a daily mousey trial.

Coconut & Velvet

Keeping the body moving is vital to its care,
With wind blowing rain sideways and puddles
    everywhere,
Motivation is what I needed, to face the daily
    chore,
Of getting out and walking fast, to somewhere
    from my door,

Thirty minutes walking sees me up by
    Canford's fields,
I cut up through the footpath, to see the view it
    yields,
As I broached the hill, I saw two dark, large
    figures stood,
They looked at me hopefully, like I might do
    them some good,

I went across to meet them and told them "I'm
    a friend,"
Silently, they let me know, their friendship
    would depend,
Upon bringing them something daily, something
    they would like,
Until that time, they wouldn't care and I could
    take a hike,

Next day wet and early, with two apples in
    my bag,
I walked again to that magic field, my feet
    I didn't drag,

There they were under a tree, sheltering from
the forces,
My friends to be, looked at me, two wet,
bedraggled horses,

They seemed to hold a conference, "shall we
leave this shelter?"
"I suspect he's brought something nice…it had
better be a belter!"
Reluctantly they sauntered over, dependency
disguised,
I showed them my old apples, both wrinkled
and shrunken-sized,

They looked at them… and then at me
… a disappointed flavour,
"We'll eat them now, but you should know,
we're doing you a favour,"
They had their snack, then turned their backs
and went back to their tree,
I said goodbye, tried to catch their eye, but
they refused to see,

I've come to know them very well and named
them for myself,
Seeing them every day has been good for all
our health,
Velvet is the female horse feisty and in charge,
Coconut is a big old boy all shaggy and nervous
and large,

I've named them for their noses, which I cup in
    feeding hand,
Coco's nose is rough and coarse, with texture
    just like sand,
Whereas Velvet's, is soft and warm, like a
    heated velvet bag,
All I know is that walking there, is not a boring
    drag.

As clouds

Clouds like puffs of pure white smoke, cross
the vast blue skies,
Lazy circling buzzard, wings outstretched, with
scanning eyes,
A rabbit sees a shadow whip across his patch of
field,
Freezes, runs for cover, crouching, panting but
concealed,

Impatient breeze pushes through the leafy tops
of trees,
Disapproving whispers filter down, to those
that take their ease,
Heavy fruit is hanging with sweet ripe
pendulous weight,
Ready to be twisted off and share a place, with
cheese upon a plate,

A ribbon stream tinkles as it threads the
grateful glens,
Fish and pebbles magnified by the clear cold
water's lens,
A plunging splash, an athletic salmon reaches
for a fly,
As clouds like puffs of pure white smoke, cross
the vast blue sky.

The English rose (to be read in a Shakespearean manner)

Moist and red, like living tissue,
The beauteous rose, upon its spindly stem doth
   sit,
From bulging bud, doth this fragrant riot issue,
In glorious English understatement, doth this
   flower fit.

For like the people of its soil,
Polite and of comely manners owned,
The beauty of the flower, the perfect foil,
To the barbed and thorny toughness there
   enthroned.

Dockleaves found nearby (written with Mum in mind)

In country law, this simple truth,
Was gifted to my curious youth,
"Where stinging nettles are all around,
Dockleaves, nearby, can be found".

This learned rustic botanical story,
Can also be an alle-gory,
For many things within life's passage,
Compare most fitting to this message.

When the sting of loss, pierces your soul,
And you feel your life, no longer whole,
Although, you won't be left unchanged,
Your path of love, will be re-arranged.

For, if love has been your life's intention,
You can always fashion its re-invention,
And when the nettle whets its sword,
A soothing leaf comes from our Lord.

Sepia dancers

The leaves will always gather in a place the
    wind can't blow,
The shapes the wind is making, the dancing
    leaves will show,
Whipping round in circles, the crunchy dancers
    wheel,
Their wafer brown-veined figures, give a sepia
    photo feel,

As quickly as they rose and danced, the wind
    removes its power,
They may dance for a second, or maybe it's an
    hour,
No trace is ever left, of this "ballroom for a
    while,"
For the leaves are blown beyond the wind and
    gather in a pile.

The daffodil

Nature's flag of green and yellow,
Signifies the dawn of spring,
Springtime and his summer fellow,
Prompt the souls of all to sing,

Waving bonnets, sway with breeze,
Bringing smiles to human faces,
Part of their role, it seems, to please,
And soften, even the hardest places.

Our sun

We call you the sun,
But, like a father you have been,
For us you are the only one,
Though a million suns can now be seen.

You light our world. You enable us to see,
You heat our world. You enable us to be,
For half of your life, now has passed,
And life you'll give us, even to your last.

Burn... burn brightly, catalyst of evolution,
Your rays can be, the death of our pollution,
For, all the power ever we needed,
Is in your heart and upon the earth that you
    have seeded.

Bee plus

Seeking and searching, buzzing, mazy flight,
From early dewy morning, till fall of cooling
   night,
The busy bee is known to "work his socks full,"
His lifetime's labour, is a jar upon our table,

What does he know of social mobility?
His life "an homage" to the Queenly nobility,
What need has he for flash cars and flashing
   money?
He flies everywhere and will only eat honey.

The robin that flutters like a leaf in the wind

The Robin that flutters like a leaf in the wind, seen from the corner of your eye and then hops into view in front of you and with feet splayed in a planted solidity, looks up at you, turning his head to allow one shining black eye to study and to question…"Have you anything for me?"

The Frog lies in the pond, four fifths hidden like a little green iceberg. He's facing away from you, but you know he can see you. It's a waiting game, do you move? If you do you risk him plopping under and diving away, scrambling under the water, longer, shorter, longer, shorter… gone now.

Magpie, formal clothing, black tie, carriages at dusk. Looks like a gentleman, but I don't think so. Makes a hell of a din. Very crow-like. When Magpies move in, the others watch out, the blackbirds have to become more openly brave, if they show weakness the Magpies will have their chicks and not for a sleep-over either.

One's for sorrow, two for joy, any more than that and it's sorrow again.

Cabbage white butterfly, "It's a pleasure to meet you, won't you stay? Oh… off you go."

You are like life itself, fleeting and hard to grasp, carried in the breeze, occasionally alighting on a flower, believing it was part of your plan, not knowing what happens next or for how long.

"I changed once, I can do it again."

Blackbird! Mr & Mrs. You are a lovely couple. She's very understated, quite ordinary-looking really, but she's a great Mum and she must have something a bit special about her because he's devoted to her and he is a very talented singer.

If Beethoven invented a car alarm it would sound like Mr. Blackbird... beautiful.

There's only one set per garden and he sings the night in...So romantic!

Autumn winds blow

Come autumn wind...blow,
Enter all the places that only you can know,
For you have blown from every angle,
And made things dance, all things that dangle,

Spiders know their circus trampoline acts,
Their web concave, web convex, web expands,
    web contracts,
Wind creating tunnel suction,
Swaying branches...hypnotic seduction,
Cause the autumn leaves to fall,
And quilt the dampened soil for all...
The tiny matchstick folk of insect culture,

Whose cold hard beetle shells are pierced by
    Vulture,
Represented in this land by little Robin beaks,
A lifetime under leaf for bugs, they lay for only
    weeks,

Blow and form the leafy mound,
A rusty island of greens, yellows, reds...all now
    browned,
Blow the winter through and hasten the revival,
Thus all living things can live, to welcome
    spring's arrival.

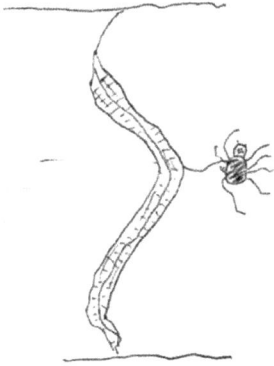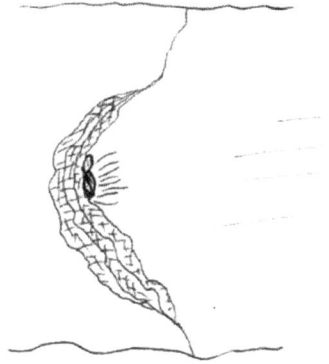

As long as the blackbirds sing

This perfect planet, has man-created woes,
The lands are dying, murdered by the men of
    kings,
We have blood on our hands and pesticide on
    our toes,
All would be well, as long as the blackbird
    sings.

Reverse the engines, focus upon the light,
Harness the wind, like an angel's mighty wings,
Reap the harvest of sea's approach and flight,
All will be well, as long as the blackbird sings.

Renounce our thirsty grasp at monetary
    growth,
And make the planet's health, your wedding
    ring,
Give up your status, although some may be
    loathe,
For all is well, as long as the blackbirds sing.

AS LONG AS
THE BLACKBIRD SINGS

Pearl

Sphere of milk-grey petrolescence, formed
    within a living creature,
Made to soften irritation's presence,
    smoothness being its primary feature,

Think of this, whilst on you read, this hidden
    treasure, smells of death,
For highly valued, this medicinal bead, to find
    it, divers hold their breath,

Millions of Oysters prised open to find, the
    pearls that will adorn a neck,
The recipient seeming not to mind, the bodies
    lying on the deck,

But, has it not always been the case, that to
    embellish the standard human form,
Has been the sacrifice of another race. A sad
    and regrettable human norm.

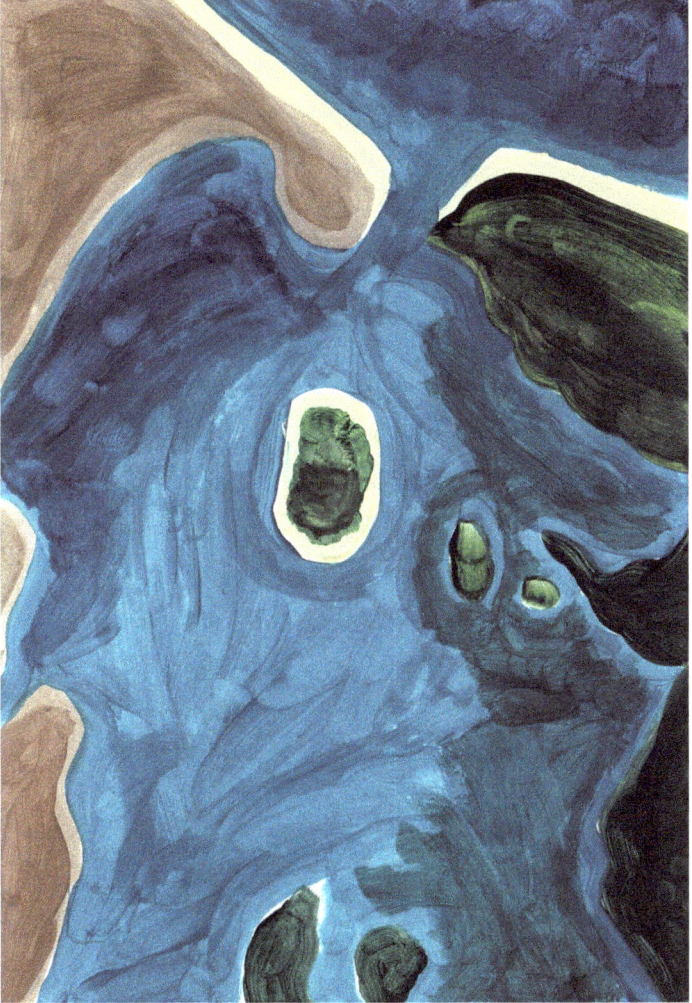

Index

Humorous poems

Prisoner 498

I'm prisoner doggie 498,
My nose is moist and my coat is great,
I'm rammed against this piece of glass,
Which, stops me reaching lush green grass.

I'm not perfect, I have my flaws,
Moulting fur, muddy paws,
I'm not aware of any crime,
Necessitating doing time.

Sure, I love to run around,
Leap for fun, cavort and bound,
Yes, I sometimes dig a hole,
Chase a bird. Catch a mole.

I am full to overflowing,
But, you are always coming…going,
Please forgive my "Joie de vivre,"
And let me out before you leave.

A war of manners

I was walking fast in the morning it was 7.04,
The pavements of Magna road, like many times
    before,
It was windy and gusty and blowing in my face,
I was wrapped up like it was Russia or some
    other freezing place,

A cyclist showed in front of me, youngish,
    around, thirty,
He was dressed in "high viz" clothing, his face
    already dirty,
I think he was a working man, who rarely takes
    a bath,
"I'm such as snob", I said to myself, with an
    under wind breath laugh,

"Morning," I called out cheery-loud, with a
    friendly greeting smile,
Nothing…as he zipped on past, my Englishness
    reviled,
My body, as if on its own, released a short
    strong fart,
And matching speed upon the wind, travelled
    like a dart,

I looked around, as I walked along, still at
    mighty pace,
The cyclist had stopped, was twisted round, a
    look upon his face,

His bitter handsome features, clearly did
  reflect,
His loathing of the skill I'd shown and maybe
  some respect,

So learn from this, anyone who is mannered
  and polite,
Some people, who we deal with, don't
  understand what's right,
The only way to interact, with those of manners
  poor,
Is to open up your bowels and say, **"stand by
  for Pooclear war."**

I am NOT Sir Isaac Newton

I was walking in the countryside, lost in
    thought, I suppose,
When an acorn from above me, bounced
    squarely on my nose,
I stood a minute, waiting for a theory to
    emerge,
I looked hopefully at the acorn, lying fallen on
    the verge,
I looked upward at the canopy of the oak,
    which I stood under,
No ground-breaking theory came along, to rip
    old science asunder,
Just a nod, to a cheeky squirrel and his very
    lucky shot,
I guess that goes to prove that... Isaac
    Newton...I am not.

I am just a fish

I am just a fish,
Swimming in the salty sea,
No ambition, no need to wish,
I am everything I need to be,

I am just a fish,
Trying hard to avoid the hook,
People would like me on a dish,
But, I have never... liked to cook.

I am just a fish.

A cup of coffee (to be read out in one breath)

Coffee, Coffee,
Hot and frothy,
Sweet as you like,
On foot, car or bike,
Sitting in your living room,
Up the feet, down the broom,
Take a sigh,
Stress, pass by,
Know you've earned one,
Body has burned one,
Eat the foam,
You're home alone,
Café coffee very nice,
Have it frappe,
That's with ice,
Use a spoon,
It's gone too soon,
Never mind, have one later,
Don't forget to tip the waiter.

An ill wind

The amount of wind that I produce,
Is akin to that of a full-grown moose,
In the home (I'm told), it's like a fog,
That has risen from a rotting bog,

It's much like having cattle loose,
White flags are raised and calls for truce,
But, I am quite unrelenting,
With my involuntary anal venting,

Spare a thought for my wife and daughter,
I know you will and I know I oughta,
But, there's little known, that I can do,
To alleviate the "Eau de Loo,"

My wife has learned to categorise,
And she names them all, as she sighs,
"Rotty botty", "bog" and "marsh,"
"Burning rubber," seems quite harsh,

She possess an amazing sense of smell,
In the world of wine, she would definitely excel,
A tragedy of romantic pairing,
With both her nostrils... and my bottom, flaring.

Lucky you

"This continual rain, is getting me down,"
Muttered the field mouse, small, damp, brown,

"It's all to do with Global Warming,"
Said a single Bee, attempting swarming,

"SOS save our souls,"
Squeaked a group of soggy moles,

From a log a small voice croaked,
"I don't mind getting soaked,"

"I quite like a marshy bog,"
Lucky you... small green frog.

Wasp

It's August now, it's time for me to fly,
My leotard still fits me... only just,
I' m craving something sweet, I don't know
    why,
I cough as my wings, stir up some dust,

Yellow and black hoops, my colour for this
    season,
I'm pleased with how look...I'm like a Bee,
But, people become Insecticidal without
    reason,
The second that I join them, for cream tea,

My cousin (a bee), never has an issue,
Even though, his body has ugly fur,
People waft him gently with a tissue,
But, when I arrive it causes quite a stir,

I do all the things, I see a Bee would do,
But, Lord, you would not believe the fuss,
A woman beating wildly with her shoe,
I'm not the crazy one, out of the two us,

I don't mind, a bit of rough and tumble,
A bit of panic, when people see it's me,
But, please respect me like you would
    a Bumble,
Don't look at me, as less than you would,
    a Bee,

My cousin gathers food in bulging knee-bags,
His buzz is no more tuneful than my own,
When he is seen, there is, cheering…bunting…
   flags,
Whereas, I feel all rejected and alone,

I get the feeling that people do not trust me,
Although, I've never hurt a living thing,
It's as easy as knowing I'm like AB…UC,
Your unkind acts will always make me sting.

My mate HEF

I have a friend, in whom I place much trust,
He's Silver–green, with just a hint of rust,
He's 17 years working... and yet.... Each year
  he is re-tyred,
He's a mover and a shaker, but only as
  required.

I feel he is my friend, as he never lets me
  down,
He always stays around me, in village or in
  town,
He can run at 90 miles per hour, or pull me up
  a hill,
I say..."I'll never let you go"...but I know some
  day I will.

He's Japanese, but, I somehow feel, he
  understands my needs,
He drinks in moderation, but very rarely feeds,
He's not good for my image, my friends have
  cooler friends,
But Hef and I have much more sense, as he
  drives me round the bends.

Index

Philosophical & Allegorical poems

The Artist

The sable tip of the old worn brush breaks the
    water's surface,
Swished around the ripple's sound, brings a
    wistful smile to her face,
Atlas splats of previous paint, adorn the artist's
    smock,
All the world can be unfurled, to the ticking of
    her clock,

The linen white of canvas bare, sits and waits
    to see,
What form its blank and vacant face, will very
    shortly be,
It knows it has potential to be a thing of beauty,
But, however it will be portrayed, is resolved to
    do its duty,

The artist, in a leap of faith, applies the early
    paint,
Like childhood, this is learning and so the
    strokes are faint,
As form is shaped and knowledge grows, the
    strokes are more defined,
And as the picture completes itself, the artist
    knows her mind,

The finished work can never be, exactly as
    desired,
For the image that was in her mind, the image
    that inspired,

Is using tools of superior make, imagination
and invention,
For human art to exceed God's own was never
God's intention.

Hybrid mind

In sleep, conscious thoughts recede into mist,
The hybrid mind, with nothing to resist,
Unconscious, now takes over at the helm,
The complex patterns play out within its realm,

The dreams of nebulous content to resolve,
Exposed, try to sweeten and dissolve,
The quandaries, that when awake, we can't
    digest,
Which, now arisen, can then be laid to rest.

All I need

All I need is to see the sky,
A circling seabird, gliding...up high,
All I need are the rustling leaves,
On the old plane tree, in the soothing breeze.

All I need is a sight of the sea,
A boat bobbing on it and a fresh fish for tea,
All I need, is nature in peace,
Its endless beauty, a bless-ed release.

All I need, is to be, in the world,
Read a good book, by the fire... I'm curled,
All I need is to be loved by those,
Who I love, in return...forgetting all woes.

Poor Hector

Handsome Paris was a Trojan prince, an archer
and a lover,
Hector was Troy's champion, a fighter and older
brother,
Together they sailed to Mycenae, where
Agamemnon ruled,
There they saw fair Helen, all caged beauty and
be-jewelled,

Helen was queen of Sparta, Menelaus her
husband and King,
He a mighty oak mature and she a sapling
thing,
Agamemnon and Menelaus were brothers of
the womb,
And oaths were sworn, to make unborn any
person whom...
...Dared to trifle with Helen.

Paris never planned ahead. Consequences
won't dull a lover,
He hid fair Helen within the boat and never told
another,
Until some leagues had passed by sail, he then
unveiled his prize,
He quickly stilled, when he saw light killed,
within strong Hector's eyes,

"My brother, you have slain us all, the people
    and the city,
The whole of Greece, will now release a storm
    that shows no pity,"
"For Achilles and his Myrmidons, the Spartan
    special forces,
Ride chariots of flame and fire, dealing death
    beneath their horses,"

Priam, wise king of Troy, looked sea-ward from
    his city,
His boys had told him what they'd done and
    he'd met the maiden pretty,
"Is this the face that launched a thousand ships?"
The prophetic question croaked slowly from his
    lips,

"I'll fight Menelaus hand to hand for the honour
    of sweet Helen's lovely hand,"
Said Paris with a flourish in an empty gesture
    grand,
"He would part your head from body, my
    foolish gentle boy,"
Said Priam, his soul now a hollow husk, bereft
    of any joy,

Achilles sat within his tent, brooding on the
    shore,
He disliked Agamemnon and disliked this civil
    war,
He would not let his cousin fight, Patroclus was
    too young,

The boy stole Achilles armour and died when
Hector's spear was flung,

Hector was astonished, when he saw whose
body died,
Fear of retribution welled up deep from his inside,
For Achilles is immortal and the fiercest of all
foes,
The focus of his God-like wrath, will double
Hector's woes,

Achilles, upon seeing his cousin, limp and
pierced and dead,
Ripped off the stolen armour and placed his
helm upon his head,
He ran towards the city, eyes on fire, his face
was fell,
Screaming "Hector"... "Hector" all the way, so
the Spartans tell,

Hector waited by the gate, as champion he
would serve,
But, when he saw Achilles, coming fast, he lost
his nerve,
Round the city, full three times, these mighty
soldiers race,
But finally Hector turned around, his final fate
to face,

They fought and none who saw this fight had
seen it's like before,
These two men, were at their peak, tempered
steel, by war,

Hector fought so valiantly, knowing as he did,
That Achilles could not die at all, like his
     younger cousin did,

Finally Hector on his knees, begged Achilles to
     stay his hand,
Patroclus's dead young body lying on the Trojan
     sand,
Achilles told poor Hector, that, dogs would eat
     his meat,
He passed his sword through Hector's neck,
     that ended him complete,

An old man came to Achilles' fire later on that
     night,
An old man, who was King Priam, sat down and
     by that light,
He talked of his sadness at the loss of his great
     son,
And begged Achilles, for the body, to do what
     must be done,

Achilles saw within his pain an echo of his own,
This mighty king had nothing now, no comfort
     in his throne,
And so the God of fighting, passed the human
     test,
And released poor Hector's body, so it could, be
     laid to rest.

The Red Poppy

Boys and men called to arms to fight and die in
    muddy trenches,
Blown to bits, or driven to fits, with cankerous
    sores and deathly stenches,
The wounded ground, disturbed and
    overturned, is fed,
With Phosphorus flares and the unburied
    compost of the rotting dead,

Now, like then, the poppies grow and replicate
    the blast of war,
With wind that blows and bends the stem and
    returns the head to where it was before,
Think hard and thank the 19th century men,
    who fought a 20th century war,
The waiters, cooks and shop assistants, who
    didn't know what was in store,

Boys, many too young to have loved, had their
    lives taken before the gun,
Cry for their mothers and know they have gone
    before they have begun,
What love awaited their return, had they but
    returned,
A library of newly written books, thrown into
    the fire and burned,

We use the poppy as a symbol of where and
   how they met their end,
The flower of a generation's youth destroyed,
   their country to defend,
It is sweet and fitting, that the flower should be
   red,
As it reminds us of the blood, those young men
   had to shed.

Goodbye and Hello

Life…when you come to analyse,
Is an endless reel of soft goodbyes,
Goodbye to childhood, hello to adult youth,
Goodbye to lullabies, hello to cold, hard truth,

Goodbye to selfish wants and needs,
Hello to marriage and selfless deeds,
Goodbye to being just we two,
Hello to little people, needing you,

Goodbye to your children, finding their own
    nest,
Hello again to freedom, though feeling not your
    best,
Goodbye to status found, when you were in
    your prime,
Hello to all the slow decay and gradual life's
    decline,

Goodbye to all potential, it's happened now… or
    never,
Hello to extra effort needed, for any small
    endeavour,
What makes it all worth it? I at last surmise,
Is… life and love and loving things…when I
    come to analyse.

Death

In our thoughts you are cloaked in black and
    soaked in all our fears,
An unwelcome guest at the end of days and the
    end of all our years,
Your arrival means the final scene, is just about
    to play,
A coachman, a ferryman, the silent travellers
    pay,

Consider this however, whoever reads this
    verse,
Death does not always travel, upon the
    crawling hearse,
For the journey from our nothingness to the
    state of being born,
Is chaperoned and possibly by the same
    unfathomable form,

So Death is Life and therefore friends, a
    different view is needed,
Maybe Death is dressed in white, when the
    foetal soul is seeded,
A faithful friend, who walks with us, between
    these unmapped places,
And fear of meeting once again, this knowledge
    fast erases.

The Oak

Mighty, the oak, unwilling servant of "great
    men's war,"
Fatally donating its flesh to fashion,
The ships, the bows, the massive castle door,
Cut and joined for the many ropes to lash-on.

Leave it! And in time your successive line will
    be shown,
A living column, a natural shade for tender
    burning skins,
With a thousand years of history quietly known,
Victories and losses and fleeting human wins.

Grizzled grey bark, furrowed tracks for busy
    insect feet,
Knots and spurs, branches gone and new ones
    in their stead,
In the moment, never thinking, only living, life
    is sweet,
Have tender tree-love, before at last **your**
    heart is dead.

Golf and life – what a game!

What a game! Contained within its 18 holes of
    luscious green,
Is every part of every life, that there has ever
    been,
Power, Judgement, patience and control,
Fortune, good or bad awaits you, on each and
    every hole,

Do you dare to smash the driver, several
    hundred yards?
Can you relax while delivering power? Will you
    hit too hard?
For although the club head must be moving, at
    100 miles per hour,
If you try to hit too hard, sweet contact will
    turn sour,

The knees must bend, the torso coil and head
    stay fully still,
Club-head withdrawn returns at pace… head
    don't move until…
Your shoulder brings your head up, the ball
    already flying,
The sailing flight, lands just right, on the
    fairway your ball is lying,

Now you must approach the green, a lofted
    iron is needed,
Your partner has just hit his well. You want to
    do what he did,

A bunker stares you in the eye. It's sandy, deep and cold,
Fly the sand-trap, attack the pin, and hope your shot is holed,

You're on the green and must assess, how the ball will roll,
Find the line, apply the pace and you may find the hole,
A smooth and pendula motion, Putter back and forth,
Allow for wind, it's blowing hard and coming from the north,

The putt is away and rolling sweetly, coming left to right,
Is it going in the hole? I really think it might,
No wait a second... it's slowing down... I think it might just stop,
One more turn. Come on ball. One more turn and drop!

Want to learn about a fellow, play with them, a round,
The deeper parts of who they are, are very quickly found,
For, as glorious and rewarding as golf can surely be,
You will find... you will know their mind... through success and adversity.

Prayer of the Sweet Pea

What is this light that shines above me?

IT IS THE SUN, MY LITTLE SWEET PEA,

Why is it there? And what does it mean?

IT BRINGS LIFE, HOPE AND WARMTH, WHEREVER IT'S SEEN,

I am a flower. What is my reason?

LIFE IS YOUR PURPOSE, THOUGH JUST FOR A SEASON,

How do I please you? What mean I to you?

YOU BRING FRAGRANT PERFUME AND COLOURS ALL HUES,

Where will I go when I finally fall?

INTO THE UNIVERSE, AS DO WE ALL,

What mark will I leave to show I was here?

A SMILE IN MY MEMORY, YOU NEED HAVE NO FEAR.

The Victorious knight

This fellow I killed had hurried here quickly,
His armour was dull, as was his defence,
I know nought of his health, perhaps he was
    sickly?
I fear that his death did not make much sense.

The killing of others has brought me plenty
    fame,
And wealth in abundance, I have here on
    display,
My family beyond me will be much the same,
My grandchildren's children will be moulded
    this way.

With wealth on the one hand and guilt on the
    other,
The blades of my sword, earthly fortunes
    anoint,
I cannot help fearing, for my soul my dear
    reader,
My sword has two edges, but only one point.

Zulu warrior

"Race for us Crispin, show all the others, what
    this gang can do,"
"I have no running shoes, my brothers, why
    choose me, not you?"
"Because you play football, every chance you
    get,"
"The most suited to be a soldier, whom I have
    ever met."

"Ok. I'll do it, for the pride of our friendship
    group,"
Before I knew it, I had joined the start line
    troupe,
In shorts and a vest and nothing on my feet,
My underdog status was now at last complete.

The field was full, the school, in force was out,
A mix of mocking and support, contained within
    the shout,
The opponents, all within my year and the year
    above,
On the line, the jostling schoolboys start to
    shove.

The pistol shot rang round the sun-scorched
    field,
The will of all, determined not to yield,
I burst away, adrenalin the food of flight,
My limbs were strong, my body, youthful light,

In the lead, I roared around the lap,
I had no need to check, the racing gap,
My bare feet, thundering as I leaned around
the bends,
A beaming face, presented to my cheering
friends.

This was it, my moment in the sun,
It ended, two minutes, from when it had
begun,
"A Zulu warrior," said my friends when
I returned,
A powerful picture, into my memory... forever...
burned.

Bournemouth Air show

Swell of people, beach-ward drawn,
Shrinking ear from shrieking child,
Red arrows flying diamond form,
Weather...sunny, dry and warm,

How many arrows are there now?
I see seven going past,
Wow! There's another! Holy Cow!
Flying low and going fast,

All of humankind is here,
Strewn across this lunar beach,
Fifty thousand...all too near,
Their skins to tan, their hair to bleach.

Memory's construct

A Mirror explodes into a thousand flying pieces,
Allows me to see angles that I've never seen,
Reveals memories from my brain's darkest
     creases,
Perspectives unknown on all that I've been.

For what are we? Any of us, but, memory's
     construct,
A vision assembled from what we will keep,
Retaining, most precious, our meritous
     conduct,
An aid to our waking and essential for sleep.

Dress rehearsal

"Come on in and take a seat. You've travelled
   quite a way,"
"We've just been looking at your life and we
   have some things to say,"
"I know this can be dis-concerting and can feel
   a bit revealing,"
"But wounds must first be looked upon, before
   we start the healing,"

"Your early life starts of course with innocent
   incomprehension,"
"Had you died at this point...well, its heavenly
   ascension,"
"As you grow and learn to lie, it's harder to gain
   admittance,"
"The things you do, as you learn to be you and
   try to save a pittance,"

"Those rules you broke and then the joke, the
   rules you then enforce,"
"The lack of care of how others fare, followed
   slowly by remorse,"
"The blindness to the basic truth, that you have
   much too many,"
"Consumer goods and exotic foods, when so
   many don't have any,"

"Do not misunderstand me, not every starving
souls' a saint,"

"Heaven is not packed with hungry people…it
definitely ain't,"

"But, those like you, who have too much, but
still don't feel their blessed,"

"Might be let in for a short time, but only as a
guest,"

"You need to work on your compassionate
feelings,"

"Be kind to others in all your earthly dealings,"

"Your learning curve must be long and very
steep,"

"Learn from this. I'm going to wake you from
your sleep."

Modern Easter contradiction

Bunnies, eggs and sweet confection,
Crucifixion…Resurrection,
Chicks and chocs and Easter trails,
Sacrifice and bloody nails.

Tasty buns with crosses on,
Signify, the forsaken son,
Sweet and sticky chocolate pleases,
Let's remember dear Lord Jesus.

The howling dogs of humanity

Rain, like medicinal balm, soothes the blistered
    ground,
Wind, cooling the hardened rock with a
    whistling, whining sound,
Like howling dogs running hard in the heat of a
    desperate chase,
Wind and water working hard on a stain they
    can't erase,

The howling dogs of humanity run wild across
    the earth,
Slashing, burning, building, turning all, to
    things of worth,
Sawing through the very branch upon which
    they stand,
Nature sharpening up the saw, to lend a
    helping hand,

The human fruit of nature's tree, has fallen and
    is rotten,
Development has taught us much, but
    something is forgotten,
The right amount to take away, is just what we
    will need,
If too much wealth is taken out, we may just
    die of greed.

The bubble

A bubble will form when elements meet,
Neither giving way, nor admitting defeat,
For one must defer and the parties combine,
Or the bubble remains, for a limited time,

The skin of the bubble, has high surface
    tension,
Refusal to mix, a sphere of dissension,
Pushing out, from within, it mustn't collapse,
It's greatest of fears, is, dilution...perhaps,

After some time, all bubbles will burst,
The contents dissolving, quite quickly at first,
What was, on the outside, is now, all there is,
From gas into liquid, plink, plink, plink, Fizz...

Broken heart (NOT based upon personal experience)

And so, at last, the heart is finally broken,
And with it, the spirit is broken too,
The painful twisted truths, at last are spoken,
The ancient wounds are opened up, anew,

The gulf between imagined and the truth,
Is seen clearly through your tear-swollen eyes,
The hope that had sustained you in your youth,
Is expunged within your heart, with all its lies,

The only course left open, is to leave,
To drag your soul away, it has been starved,
To sit in isolation and to grieve,
And live the life that's left, as two lives halved.

The heart

Heavy is the load for the heart that is full of
   dreary regret,
Heavy is the weight of the spirit of the soul that
   will not forget,
All the petty misdemeanours perpetrated by
   "the other,"
And fails to see all as sister, father, mother,
   brother,

A heart that is full of love for the generous life
   that has been given,
Is not a smoky, choking organ, which has been
   riven,
It is a heart that's light and ticks with rhythmic
   love,
For all the miraculous people, none of whom
   we are above.

To Chris over the road (in memory of Glyn)

I write this poem to you, with love,
I hope that it will help you through,
A low-point time, to rise above,
With knowledge that, there is love for you,

A good man has been your rock,
Throughout your adult life…till now,
And comfy, like a favourite sock,
You have been, since marriage vow,

You must continue to walk the road,
That previously you walked with Glyn,
But, not alone you'll bear the load,
For we are near you…and always in.

Falling

I'm falling from a height so great,
A height I dare not estimate,
Time moved slowly at the start of fall,
It took time to comprehend it all,
The earth seemed distant and in its natural
    place,
The air was thin, gentle zephyrs on my face,
My arms and legs out-stretched to form a star,
The world was growing slowly, still small and
    round and far,
I've spent some time, along the way, slowing
    my descent,
Knowing all along, that nothing can prevent,
The eventual combination of man and solid
    ground,
But in the years of falling, this is what I've
    found...

Let kindness be your intention and try to do
    what's right,
Everything you give to love, can only gain you
    height,
Complete descent is guaranteed, no matter
    what you do,
So, float as gently as you can, make good the
    real you.

Perspective

As the sun rises, the sun will also set,
On this brightly-coloured spinning marble in a
    sea of infinite Jett,
All the boundaries drawn and battles fought,
All the Colours, beliefs and Religions taught,
All the great creations and inventions and
    intentions, the universe will forget,
As the sun rises, the sun will also set.

Life (a take on it)

Life is like fire, the sparks of which, did not
   start here,
Flying through space as bugs, on rocks of ice,
Evolving into animals, upon this Earthy sphere,
The soul is the fire. The body is just a device.

The lifetime of the creature is the burning of
   the wood,
And when the wood is burned, the sparks fly
   on,
The hope is that the soul has gathered good,
As the fire of one, is the fire of many, before
   it's gone.

The spark is tempered by the fire, it has been,
And when the planet of the forest has been
   used,
The sparks, return to space, so vast, unseen,
To find a place to burn, once more…infused.

This theory doesn't change our God's
   existence,
The complexity of all things implies, it's true,
I understand, why knowledge breeds
   resistance,
The question is… "Does **your** God, walk with
   you?"

Happy contradiction

To be young, with future not yet known,

To be adult, though not in every way
   full-grown,

To know, what it takes a lifetime to learn,

To carry full knowledge, without full concern,

To live a whole life in this happy state,

To know your world, before it's too late,

To be the carefree spirit of youth,

To be young and carry maturity's truth.

Goodness is its own reward

By design, we're wired to think,
Our actions work on "tit for tat,"
Do a good thing, receive a drink,
Do a bad thing, eat a mat,

But, in real life, it's not that straight,
In your car let someone out,
Then it's your turn...sit and wait,
Don't get angry, fume or pout,

The world is complex and very busy,
The good you do, is small in size,
Injustice must not make you fizzy,
Just give goodness and be wise,

For even though, it seems unfair,
The discourteousness we can receive,
Full of goodness and of care,
Its own reward, I do believe.

Grateful for less

The comfort of wealth can easily blunt, a young
person's ambition,
If one is not under fire, then why would one
make ammunition?
A tutor can help young Hector to rise in his
class,
I know it's a bore, but the job that awaits,
needs a pass.

Privilege is fraught with dangerous behavioural
defects,
Dissatisfied with more, entitled, society's
prefects,
Spoiled, by a lack of simple daily friction,
Bored and tired, but all with impeccable diction,

If every day is hard and a struggle to make
ends meet,
The character that emerges is more likely to be
complete,
For pain is seen and felt and it's therefore
understood,
That being grateful for less will make a life feel
good.

The thrill of creation

How can it be? That creatures, so full of God's
   creative light,
Can come from dawn, so quickly to the night,
To paint the way that Leonardo da Vinci did,
So rapidly, the painting pot, is re-covered by
   the lid,

To sing as only Pavarotti could,
To scale the heights angelic, with a voice that
   always should,
Be heard forever more, through space and
   time,
"All shall sleep" is the celestial paradigm,

To write the way that Shakespeare used to
   write,
His allocated span, only half of his twelfth
   night,
"To be or not to be?" Well... I would say...
   he was,
The greatest of all time, there's no because,

To get perspective, one must not forget,
As the sun rises, the sun will also set,
And to thine own self, one must, always be
   true,
For creation's thrill, is life inside of you.

<u>Give, not to receive and you will be given to</u>

He pours his humour over, things that are too
    dry,
He makes them taste much better and he helps
    the day pass by,
He always hopes to raise a smile. He likes to
    make folk laugh,
When things are done with laughter, the load is
    cut by half.

Do not mistake the light approach, for someone
    who is light,
When forced to take a firmer stance, he will
    always fight,
But fighting and coercing are not his natural
    way,
And he will walk the long way round, if that will
    save the day.

For, love for all, is in his heart, he cares how
    you are feeling,
This is not an easy life, for some are
    double-dealing,
But, strong is he, who goes through life and
    doesn't carry armour,
Calm and pure and happy is he, who donates
    all to Karma.

"To thine own self be true"

Remember this above all else…"To thine own
    self be true",
A portrait of wisdom, drawn by Stratford's
    bard,
It is easier to talk of, than it is to do,
But all things of worth are destined to be hard.

It does not mean, do what you must,
Although that may be good for mental health,
The real point, in which we duly trust,
Is do not lie to, or deceive yourself.

Vanity can distort your self-review,
Perverting the image in your mirror-mind,
If your judgement unimpaired be true?
By truth at last, some peace I hope you'll find.

Index

For Mum and in memory of Dad

Happy 81st birthday (Walk the line Mum)

I'm very proud of how well you seem,
You still have vision and scope to dream,
You are not stilted or old like some,
You walk the line, walk the line Mum.

The birds and flowers are friends to you,
Your love of life is still quite new,
Your inner child un-dimmed by time,
Walk the line Mum, walk the line.

The line is keeping keen and busy,
The line is stopping before you're dizzy,
The line is living with time to come,
You walk the line, walk the line Mum. X

(Now 87 and still walking the line).

Cedar wood

This shed is made of Cedar wood, which
    means, it will not rot,
This reminds me of my dear old Mum, the Mum
    that time forgot,
For like that shed, my Mum is made of pretty
    rugged stuff,
But, unlike that old Cedar shed, her edges are
    not rough,

I Cedar only just last week, sawing off some
    branches,
Like one of those tough frontier wives, you see
    sometimes on ranches,
I Cedar last year moving tiles, over a hundred
    needed,
My efforts to make her walk the line... often are
    not heeded,

I Cedar point however...if you keep the body
    moving,
Your health is boosted by the use and blood
    pressure's improving,
I Cedar benefit also of, continuous home
    improvement,
It's stimulating to the brain and helps with
    healthy movement.

John (through Mary's eyes)

An innocent, I was to manly ways,
In a time, post-war, of charming, simpler days,
A friend of a friend, when first we met,
Your smile lit your face in a way I can't forget.

Tall and straight, a man you were full grown,
You won my heart, which to this day, you own,
Sophisticated, to my starry eyes,
We talked of things and love wore no disguise.

From one, to two and then to five,
Our love had brought our sons alive,
And all the way from there to here,
You're everything I hold most dear.

Yet another word from the author

Thank you for buying and for reading this slightly self-indulgent book of poetry and of art.

I hope you enjoyed the art from my family members as much as I have over the years.

My motivation for nearly all of the poems within this book, came from wanting to call round at my Mum's with something to read to her, which she would enjoy. She has always enjoyed seeing her sons do something competently, successfully and happily.

By putting these poems into a book, beautifully supported by the pictures created by my Mum, my lovely wife and my two beautiful daughters, I feel I have created something for them to appreciate now and in time to come.

Finally, it is unlikely that a book of this nature will achieve massive financial or critical success. By self-publishing, I have succeeded in achieving what I aimed to do.

As long as I have the motivation of my Mum to visit and impress (and please), I will continue to write a poem every week and that might amount to volume 2 sometime in the future.

Thank you again.
With Love,

Crispin

www.ingramcontent.com/pod-product-compliance
Lightning Source LLC
Chambersburg PA
CBHW052129150426

42813CB00077B/2646